Crypto Foundations For Building Multi-Generational Wealth

GMB GROW MY BAG™
WHERE INVESTORS CONNECT. ENGAGE. THRIVE.

Book layout and design by Helayne Friedland.
Cover art by Agon Shehu.

*This book is dedicated
to my whole family,
but especially my four Toonkies.*

◆

They are the air I breathe.

⬡ Table of Contents

⬡ Introduction

"Crypto Foundations—For Building Multi-Generational Wealth" is a comprehensive guide that unlocks the vast potential of cryptocurrency for wealth building across generations. This book demystifies the origins of crypto, and illuminates Bitcoin's unparalleled status while providing an accessible introduction to altcoins, enriched by real-world case studies, and clarifies the distinctions between tokens and coins—covering utility tokens, security tokens, and the pivotal role of stablecoins.

As you navigate through the digital age, this book serves as your compass, exploring cutting-edge concepts like Web3, the Metaverse, NFTs, and the principles of decentralization. It provides an in-depth understanding of the infrastructure supporting blockchain and cryptocurrencies, the emerging Semantic Web, and the transformative power of AI and machine learning.

"Crypto Foundations" also delves into the technical realm of interoperability and the immersive experiences of virtual, augmented, and extended reality, advocating for user sovereignty. With an emphasis on risk management and portfolio diversification, it guides readers through the nuances of cryptocurrency investing, from the fundamentals of risk management principles to integrating cryptocurrencies into a broader investment portfolio.

This book offers a forward-looking perspective on decentralized finance, decentralized physical infrastructure networks (DPINs), and the tokenization revolution. It presents a robust investment analysis framework for cryptocurrencies, comparing traditional banks with cryptocurrency exchanges, and charts the evolution from plastic to digital payment systems, highlighting the ascendancy of cryptocurrency.

Complete with an overview of exchanges, both centralized and decentralized, and a deep dive into security, regulation, and the spectrum of wallets, "Crypto Foundations" empowers readers with the knowledge to make informed investment choices. Whether you're directly investing or building on a solid foundation, this book is an indispensable resource for anyone looking to navigate the complex, promising world of cryptocurrency and build multi-generational wealth.

Bitcoin's birth spurred a frenzy of innovatior
with altcoins like Litecoin, Ripple, and Ethereu.
something new to the table. Ethereum introduced .
expanding on Bitcoin's foundation.

Blockchain, the tech underpinning Bitcoin, quickly gained .
for its potential beyond just currency. Its appeal lies in its abil
transparency, security, and decentralization. Suddenly, industries ι
healthcare to supply chain management began eyeing blockchain as .
solution to age-old problems.

The rise of Bitcoin and its crypto descendants has fundamentally
shifted our perspective on money, privacy, and the power structures
of the Internet. Cryptocurrencies have thrown down the gauntlet to
traditional financial systems, offering a new way of thinking about global
transactions, inclusivity, and resistance to censorship.

From the early cryptographic experiments to Bitcoin's emergence and
the subsequent wave of altcoins and blockchain applications, the journey
of cryptocurrency is a testament to the power of innovation and the
enduring quest for a decentralized solution to digital challenges. This is
more than just a financial revolution; it is a reimagining of what currency
can be in the digital age.

Bitcoin's Unique Position

Embarking on an exploration into the Bitcoin saga, the linchpin of the
cryptocurrency universe. Cast your mind back to 2008, a groundbreaking
year when an enigmatic figure or group known as Satoshi Nakamoto
unveiled the Bitcoin whitepaper. This wasn't just a technical document;
it was a manifesto for a new era of finance, proposing a decentralized
system for electronic transactions, free from the constraints of trust-
based models. Fast forward to February 17, 2024, and Bitcoin has
ascended to a market capitalization of an astonishing $1.02 trillion USD,
establishing itself as the behemoth of the digital currency world.

Bitcoin's gravitational pull in the Cryptoverse is unparalleled.
Commanding about 43% of the total cryptocurrency market cap, its

The Origins of Crypto

Diving into the world of cryptocurrency feels like opening a door to the future, a journey that began with a simple yet revolutionary idea: secure digital communication using cryptographic techniques. The path to creating a decentralized digital currency was no short sprint; it was a marathon that spanned decades, filled with cryptographers and computer scientists dreaming big before Bitcoin ever made headlines.

Let's roll back to the 1980s and 1990s, a time when the Internet was just finding its feet. Researchers were playing around with cryptographic protocols, laying down the groundwork for what would eventually become secure digital transactions. Then came DigiCash in the 1990s, created by David Chaum. It was an ambitious early attempt at digital money, promising privacy through cryptography. Though DigiCash didn't quite hit the mark commercially, it was a trailblazer, showing us what could be possible.

In the shadows of these developments, visionaries like Wei Dai with B-Money and Nick Szabo with Bit Gold started floating ideas about a decentralized digital currency. Their projects weren't fully realized, but they planted seeds that would grow into the towering tree of cryptocurrency we see today.

2008 was a watershed year. Someone, or perhaps a group, under the pseudonym Satoshi Nakamoto, dropped the Bitcoin whitepaper. This wasn't just another academic paper; it was a blueprint for a new world of finance. "Bitcoin: A Peer-to-Peer Electronic Cash System" proposed a currency system that didn't need central authorities to prevent double-spending, thanks to a clever proof-of-work mechanism.

By January 2009, the Bitcoin network flickered to life. Nakamoto mined the very first block, embedding a headline from The Times as both a timestamp and a critique of the financial system of the time. It was a quiet revolution, but the first Bitcoin transaction sent ripples through the digital realm, signaling the dawn of the first functioning cryptocurrency.

influence is colossal, shaping not just market dynamics but also investor sentiment across the board. Bitcoin's price movements ripple through the crypto market, setting trends and dictating flows, though it is fascinating to observe how this correlation has begun to diversify as the market matures.

The ripple effect of Bitcoin extends beyond the Cryptoverse, subtly influencing traditional financial markets, albeit without causing significant upheaval. Yet, its role as a bastion of investor confidence is unmistakable. Regarded as a relatively secure entry point into the volatile world of cryptocurrencies, Bitcoin has magnetized both institutional and individual investors, enhancing the legitimacy and stability of the entire crypto ecosystem.

However, the journey isn't devoid of hurdles. Bitcoin grapples with issues such as high transaction fees and scalability challenges, which have sparked debates about its suitability for mass adoption. Amidst this, a new generation of cryptocurrencies has emerged, armed with innovative solutions to these enduring problems, challenging Bitcoin's supremacy.

Despite these challenges, the towering stature and influence of Bitcoin within the crypto realm are indisputable. It has not only charted the course for the evolution of digital currencies but also revolutionized our conceptualization of financial transactions, privacy, and autonomy.

Bitcoin's story is interwoven with discussions about the integration of cryptocurrencies into broader financial and regulatory frameworks. Its ascent has catalyzed a wave of innovation, drawing the gaze of regulatory bodies worldwide and fueling debates on cryptocurrency's place in future monetary systems. Simultaneously, it has laid the technological and philosophical foundation for the plethora of altcoins and blockchain projects that followed, each endeavoring to expand upon or refine the revolutionary ideals of decentralization, transparency, and immutability that Bitcoin introduced.

In wrapping up this exploration of Bitcoin's monumental impact, it is evident that its legacy transcends its market cap or technological achievements. Bitcoin has fundamentally shifted the paradigm of financial transactions, challenging traditional notions of money and authority. As we look towards the horizon, the landscape is vibrant with potential and challenges alike. Bitcoin's pioneering spirit continues to inspire a future where finance is democratized, and the dreams of a decentralized world inch closer to reality. The narrative of Bitcoin is far from concluded; it is a saga that continues to unfold, promising a journey of innovation, adaptation, and transformation in the ever-evolving world of cryptocurrency.

Introduction to Altcoins

Venturing beyond the pioneering footsteps of Bitcoin, we delve into the vibrant world of altcoins—alternative cryptocurrencies that emerged in Bitcoin's wake, bringing innovation, addressing Bitcoin's challenges, or exploring new applications of blockchain technology. Altcoins are not mere shadows of Bitcoin; they're trailblazers in their own right, each contributing uniquely to the blockchain ecosystem.

Utility tokens unlock the doors to blockchain-powered services, offering access to the functionalities within various projects. Ethereum's Ether (ETH) is a prime example, serving not just as a digital currency but as the vital energy that powers the Ethereum network's smart contracts and decentralized applications (DApps). This utility extends the blockchain's reach beyond financial transactions, enabling a universe of decentralized solutions.

Security tokens merge the blockchain with traditional assets, digitizing ownership of real-world assets like stocks or real estate. They're a bridge between the old and new financial worlds, offering investment returns with an added layer of regulatory security. It's a concept that redefines what digital ownership entails, bringing tangible assets into the digital realm.

Stablecoins stand as the steadying force in the cryptocurrency market's tumultuous seas. Anchored to stable assets like fiat currencies, stablecoins aim to marry cryptocurrency's innovative transactional capabilities with the reliability of traditional currency values. Tether (USDT) and USD Coin (USDC) exemplify this blend, striving to offer stability in a notoriously volatile space.

Ethereum has been a game-changer, introducing the world to smart contracts and DApps. It's a platform that transcends financial transactions, allowing developers to create decentralized solutions for everything from finance (DeFi) to art (NFTs), making Ethereum a pivotal platform for blockchain innovation.

Ripple (XRP) aims to streamline global payments, making cross-border transactions as simple as sending an email. By focusing on reducing transaction times and costs, Ripple positions itself as a modern alternative to traditional financial systems like SWIFT, promising a future of efficient global money movement.

Litecoin, often referred to as the silver to Bitcoin's gold, sought to improve Bitcoin's model by enabling faster transactions accessible to individual miners. It's tailored for daily transactions, offering an appealing option for cryptocurrency use in everyday life.

Cardano differentiates itself with a research-driven approach, emphasizing a layered blockchain architecture for improved scalability and security. It aims to foster a sustainable ecosystem with diverse applications, from finance to education, grounded in academic rigor and research.

Solana distinguishes itself with its high-speed blockchain capabilities, thanks to its innovative Proof of History (PoH) combined with Proof of Stake (PoS). This allows for rapid transaction processing, making Solana a go-to platform for developers and supporting a wide range of DApps, from DeFi platforms to NFT marketplaces. Solana's commitment to speed, scalability, and a developer-friendly environment underscores its role as a key player in the blockchain revolution, pushing the boundaries of what's possible in decentralized applications and services.

As we wrap up this exploration, it is clear that altcoins have significantly broadened the horizons of the cryptocurrency world. They've introduced a future where blockchain technology is foundational not only for financial transactions but to an expansive array of digital interactions and services. With each altcoin carving out its niche, they collectively push forward the narrative of decentralized finance and digital ownership, marking an exciting era in the evolution of blockchain technology.

Case Studies

In the vast and varied world of cryptocurrencies, several key players have carved out niches that both complement and enhance the blockchain ecosystem beyond Bitcoin's foundational role. Let's dig into a few of these trailblazers—Ethereum, Ripple, Litecoin, Solana, Chainlink, and Cardano—each of which has introduced unique innovations and applications that underscore the potential of blockchain technology.

Ethereum, often hailed as the decentralized application powerhouse, brought the concept of smart contracts into the limelight. These self-executing contracts, written in code, have opened up a new realm of possibilities, from decentralized finance (DeFi) platforms to non-fungible token (NFT) marketplaces. With its ongoing transition to Ethereum 2.0, which adopts a Proof of Stake (PoS) consensus mechanism, Ethereum is on a path to achieving greater scalability and energy efficiency, ensuring its place as a cornerstone of blockchain-based applications.

Ripple has made waves by streamlining global financial transactions. Its unique consensus mechanism bypasses the cumbersome and costly traditional banking systems, facilitating rapid and cost-effective cross-border payments. RippleNet, Ripple's answer to the outdated SWIFT system, offers a sleek, modern approach to international money transfers, supporting fiat currencies, cryptocurrencies, and even commodities.

Litecoin emerged as a "light" version of Bitcoin, aiming for faster transaction confirmations and a mining algorithm that's more inclusive for individual miners. It positions itself as an ideal solution for everyday transactions, providing a faster and more efficient alternative for payments and transfers.

Solana has quickly gained recognition for its remarkable transaction speed and scalability, thanks to its innovative Proof of History (PoH) and Proof of Stake (PoS) mechanisms. This efficiency makes it a favored platform for developers, supporting a wide range of high frequency decentralized applications, from DeFi to gaming, and showcasing the potential for blockchain to handle operations at scale.

Chainlink bridges the gap between blockchains and the real world by providing reliable, real-time data to smart contracts through its decentralized oracle network. This functionality enables more complex and practical applications of blockchain technology, where real-world information is crucial for execution.

Cardano differentiates itself with a strong emphasis on a research-first approach, sustainability, scalability, and interoperability. With a unique two-layer architecture, it separates the processes of settlement and computation, allowing for more sophisticated transactions and smart contract functionalities. Cardano's vision extends to creating a more secure and scalable blockchain infrastructure with applications across various sectors, including education, retail, and finance.

These case studies highlight the incredible diversity and innovation within the cryptocurrency space. From Ethereum's foundational platform for smart contracts and DApps to Ripple's efficient payment network, Litecoin's quick transactions, Solana's scalability, Chainlink's real-world connectivity, and Cardano's sustainable design, each project contributes uniquely to the evolution of blockchain technology. Together, they expand on Bitcoin's legacy, pushing the boundaries of what's possible and paving the way for a future where blockchain technology plays a leading role in our digital and financial lives.

Tokens vs. Coins—Utility Tokens, Security Tokens, and Stablecoins

Now, let's review the fascinating world of cryptocurrencies, where the terms "coins," "tokens," and "stablecoins" are more than just buzzwords. They are the key players in the digital currency universe, each with its unique role and purpose. Understanding these distinctions is like unlocking a treasure chest of knowledge, revealing the depth and diversity of the crypto ecosystem.

Imagine coins as the pioneers of the cryptocurrency world. They're like the digital equivalent of the money in your wallet but exist on their own unique blockchains. Bitcoin, for example, not only kicked off the crypto revolution but continues to dominate as a digital currency, used for everything from buying a coffee to serving as an investment. Then there's Ethereum's Ether, which adds another layer of utility by fueling smart contracts and applications on its network, showing us just how multifaceted coins can be.

Now, let's talk about tokens, the versatile tools that serve multiple purposes across the blockchain landscape. Unlike coins, tokens operate on existing blockchains and can represent anything from a piece of art to voting rights in a decentralized organization. They're the Swiss army knives of the crypto world, offering a range of functionalities that extend beyond the basic concept of currency. Whether it is rewarding users for their attention online, representing a share in a real estate project, or allowing participation in the governance of a decentralized protocol, tokens illustrate the innovative ways blockchain technology is being applied today.

In the midst of crypto's notorious price swings, stablecoins stand out as the calming force, tethered to stable assets like the dollar to keep their value steady. They merge the best of both worlds: the efficiency and security of cryptocurrencies and the predictable value of fiat currencies. This stability is a game-changer for those looking to use digital currency without the rollercoaster ride of traditional crypto prices.

As we explore these concepts further, we encounter coins like Litecoin, designed for faster, more lightweight transactions, and Ethereum's Ether, which powers a whole ecosystem of decentralized applications. On the token side, we have examples like DAI, a stablecoin that shields users from volatility, Chainlink, which bridges the gap between blockchains and real-world data, and Uniswap's UNI, empowering users to have a say in the exchange's future.

In wrapping up this journey through the Cryptoverse, it is clear that the distinction between coins and tokens isn't just semantic; it reflects the rich tapestry of possibilities that cryptocurrencies and blockchain technology bring to the table. From the transactional bedrock provided by coins to the expansive utility of tokens and the stabilizing presence of stablecoins, the crypto world is a dynamic and evolving space. As we move forward, understanding these differences is crucial for anyone looking to navigate the nuances of the crypto ecosystem and harness its vast potential. The future of finance and digital services is being rewritten, promising a landscape that's more inclusive, transparent, and decentralized than ever before.

The Story of Stablecoins

Stablecoins emerge as the crypto ecosystem's strategic solution to counterbalance the notorious volatility that characterizes digital currencies like Bitcoin and Ethereum. These digital currencies are ingeniously tethered to more stable assets—commonly fiat currencies such as the US dollar, the euro, or commodities like gold—to maintain a consistent value over time. This anchoring mechanism is what sets stablecoins apart, providing a bridge between the unpredictable nature of cryptocurrencies and the reliability of traditional financial assets.

At their core, stablecoins aim to combine the best of both worlds: the swift, borderless transactions and digital convenience of cryptocurrencies with the predictable, stable value of fiat currencies. This fusion results in a digital asset that's well-suited for daily transactions, remittances, and serving as a safe haven for traders and investors looking to escape the wild price swings of the crypto market.

The underlying technology of stablecoins can vary, with some relying on collateralized assets held in reserve—such as cash or short-term government securities—to back each token, while others are algorithmically stabilized through smart contracts that manage the supply of the issued stablecoin to maintain its peg.

The appeal of stablecoins extends beyond mere stability; they also promise enhanced efficiency in financial transactions. They facilitate faster, cheaper, and more transparent payments and transfers, not just within the cryptocurrency space but also in traditional finance and global commerce. This makes them particularly useful for cross-border transactions, where they can significantly reduce costs and settlement times compared to conventional banking systems.

Moreover, stablecoins are instrumental in the burgeoning field of decentralized finance (DeFi), where they serve as a predictable medium of exchange, lending, and earning interest without the involvement of traditional financial intermediaries. This utility underscores the transformative potential of stablecoins, not just as a hedge against volatility, but as foundational elements for innovative financial services and products.

In summary, stablecoins stand as a testament to the innovative spirit of the cryptocurrency world, offering a stable, efficient, and versatile digital currency option. Their growing adoption across various sectors underscores their potential to not only mitigate the challenges of crypto volatility but also to redefine the future of financial transactions and services.

⬡ Web3

Web 3.0, frequently termed the third generation of the Internet or simply Web3, signifies a pivotal evolution in the digital realm, focusing on principles of decentralization, blockchain technologies, and a token-based economy. This iteration of the web builds upon the foundational, static content of Web 1.0 and the rich, interactive, social capabilities that emerged with Web 2.0. Web3 introduces an advanced layer of functionality and interactivity, underpinned by several core features that aim to redefine user experience on the Internet.

Central to Web3 is the concept of decentralization, which seeks to distribute the control and storage of data across numerous nodes in a network rather than centralizing it in the hands of a few entities. This shift is facilitated by blockchain technology, which underpins cryptocurrencies and enables secure, transparent transactions without the need for intermediary institutions. Blockchain's inherent security and transparency features are poised to revolutionize not just financial transactions but also identity verification, supply chain management, and more, by enabling smart contracts and decentralized applications (dApps).

Moreover, Web3 is distinguished by its use of a token-based economy, where digital assets and utilities are tokenized to represent ownership or membership rights within the digital space. This approach not only democratizes access to digital content and services but also provides a new model for creators and consumers to interact directly, bypassing traditional gatekeepers.

Another groundbreaking aspect of Web3 is its emphasis on semantic web technologies, which aim to make Internet data machine-readable, thereby enhancing the accuracy of content discovery and the relevance of user interactions. Coupled with the integration of artificial intelligence and machine learning, Web3 is set to deliver more personalized, intuitive online experiences.

Extended Reality (XR) technologies, including Virtual Reality (VR), Augmented Reality (AR), and Mixed Reality (MR), are also integral to the

Web3 vision, offering immersive experiences that blur the lines between the physical and digital worlds. These technologies extend the scope of the web beyond traditional screens, promising new paradigms for gaming, education, remote work, and social interactions.

Unlike Web 2.0, which was characterized by the rise of social networks and user-generated content, Web3 doesn't seek to replace its predecessor but rather to augment and enhance the digital experience by addressing some of the Internet's current limitations, such as data privacy concerns, reliance on central authorities, and the equitable distribution of value across users and creators. By embedding trust into the very fabric of the Internet and empowering users with greater control over their data and digital identities, Web3 represents not just a technological shift but also a cultural and economic one, promising a more open, connected, and user-centric Internet.

In summary, Web3 embodies the next stage in the Internet's evolution, driven by a commitment to decentralization, enhanced security, user empowerment, and immersive technologies. Its development heralds a future where digital interactions are more transparent, equitable, and engaging, heralding a significant transformation in how we live, work, and connect online.

Metaverse

Imagine a digital universe, an expansive network of interconnected virtual spaces where the boundaries between the physical and digital worlds blur. This is the vision of the metaverse, a term that captures the essence of the future Internet. It is a realm where virtual reality (VR), augmented reality (AR), and other cutting-edge technologies merge to create immersive environments for users to live, work, and play.

The metaverse is not a monolith. Contrary to the singular worlds depicted in science fiction, the metaverse comprises a patchwork of virtual experiences and platforms, each developed by different entities. This diversity is what makes the metaverse a dynamic concept, evolving with each technological advancement and creative endeavor. From virtual marketplaces and concert venues to digital offices and art galleries, the metaverse is shaping up to be a multifaceted ecosystem of social and economic interactions.

At the heart of the metaverse lies the desire to connect. Whether it is through attending a concert performed by a favorite artist in a virtual venue, exploring an exhibition in a digital museum, conducting a business meeting across continents in a shared virtual space, or simply having a virtual hangout with friends, the metaverse promises new dimensions of social interaction and connectivity. It is a vision of a future where experiences are not limited by physical constraints, offering a new level of immersion and engagement.

The building blocks of the metaverse are as varied as its potential applications. While VR and AR are often spotlighted as the gateways to these immersive worlds, the foundation of the metaverse is much broader. Technologies such as artificial intelligence (AI) play a role in creating responsive, dynamic environments and characters. Blockchain technology introduces new possibilities for digital ownership and economy, enabling users to buy, sell, and trade virtual goods with real-world value. Meanwhile, the Internet of Things (IoT) integrates physical data into digital spaces, enriching the metaverse with information from the physical world.

Yet, for all its promise, the metaverse is still in its infancy. The vision of a fully realized, interconnected digital universe faces significant hurdles. Accessibility remains a challenge, with advanced hardware often required to experience the most immersive aspects of the metaverse. Issues of interoperability, where different virtual spaces and platforms seamlessly connect, are yet to be fully resolved. Moreover, ensuring user security and privacy in these new digital frontiers is paramount.

In summary, the metaverse represents an exciting frontier in the evolution of the Internet and digital technology. It is a burgeoning universe of possibility, where digital and physical realities converge to create new forms of interaction, entertainment, and work. Yet, as we stand on the brink of this new digital era, it is important to approach with both enthusiasm and caution. The path to realizing the full potential of the metaverse is complex and uncharted, requiring innovation, collaboration, and a careful consideration of the ethical implications of these new virtual worlds. As we venture into these digital landscapes, the journey promises to be as transformative as it is uncertain, reshaping our digital and physical realities in ways we are only beginning to imagine.

NFTs

Let's delve into the fascinating world of Non-Fungible Tokens (NFTs) and their integral role in shaping the next generation of the Internet, Web3. NFTs are more than just a digital trend; they represent a fundamental shift in how we perceive and interact with digital assets. These unique digital tokens exist on a blockchain, the bedrock of Web3, providing a decentralized ledger that records ownership and transactions.

What sets NFTs apart is their distinct nature. Unlike cryptocurrencies such as Bitcoin or Ethereum, which are interchangeable or "fungible," each NFT is one-of-a-kind. This uniqueness allows them to serve as digital certificates of ownership for a wide array of assets, be it a piece of digital art, a music track, a video clip, or even parcels of virtual land. For artists, musicians, and creators, NFTs have opened new doors to digital scarcity and ownership, enabling them to monetize their work directly in a way that wasn't possible before.

At the heart of NFTs lies the principle of decentralization. Since they're stored on decentralized blockchains, control is distributed across the network rather than held by a single authority. This decentralization aligns perfectly with Web3's vision of a user-centric Internet, free from the constraints and control of centralized entities. It empowers users and creators, giving them control over their digital assets and interactions.

Another cornerstone of NFTs is interoperability. Built on standard protocols, NFTs can traverse across various dApps, platforms, and marketplaces without being locked into a single ecosystem. This fluidity enhances the user experience, allowing digital assets to be more widely used and integrated into the broader digital world of Web3.

NFTs also redefine economic models, particularly for the creative industry. By tokenizing digital content, creators can directly sell their work to a global audience, fostering a new economy that values digital content in its own right. This model cuts out intermediaries, ensuring that creators receive a fairer share of the profits.

Moreover, NFTs have become focal points for digital communities and social engagement. Many NFT projects cultivate vibrant communities where members not only invest in digital assets but also participate in governance, events, and discussions. This community-driven approach reinforces Web3's emphasis on collaboration and shared governance.

NFTs are a testament to the transformative potential of Web3. They are pioneering a new era of digital ownership, economic models, and community engagement. By enabling true digital scarcity, interoperability, and decentralized control, NFTs are at the forefront of reimagining what digital assets can be. As we venture deeper into the Web3 landscape, NFTs stand as beacons of innovation, illustrating the vast possibilities of a decentralized, user-owned Internet.

Decentralization

Diving into the essence of Web3, we encounter a transformative concept at its core: decentralization. This isn't just a buzzword; it is a paradigm shift from the centralized structures that dominate the current Internet landscape. Web3 embodies the transition to a network where power and control are distributed across its users, rather than being concentrated in the hands of a few large entities.

At the heart of this decentralized vision is blockchain technology. Imagine a world where your data isn't stored on a single server owned by a massive corporation but is instead spread out across a vast network of computers, each holding a piece of the puzzle. This is the foundation of blockchain, a ledger that is not only transparent but incredibly difficult to tamper with. It ensures that transactions, whether they're financial or data exchanges, are secure, verifiable, and, most importantly, not under the control of any single entity.

The implications of decentralization are profound. For starters, it hands back control to users over their personal data. In today's digital age, data is currency, and under a decentralized model, you have the sovereignty to decide how and with whom your data is shared. This model challenges the status quo, where big tech companies harvest and monetize user data with little to no compensation for the individuals it belongs to.

Decentralization also fosters a more democratic and equitable Internet. By eliminating central points of control, it paves the way for more open and accessible platforms where censorship is harder to enforce, and innovation can thrive without gatekeepers. It's about creating a more resilient Internet, where services and platforms can run uninterrupted, even if parts of the network go down.

Moreover, decentralization redefines trust in digital interactions. Instead of placing trust in a company or an intermediary, trust is built into the architecture of the blockchain through its consensus mechanisms and encryption. This not only makes transactions more secure but also opens new possibilities for direct peer-to-peer interactions, without the need for intermediaries.

In summary, decentralization is the bedrock upon which Web3 is built. It represents a shift towards a more open, secure, and user-empowered Internet. By leveraging blockchain technology, Web3 aims to dismantle the centralized powers that currently dominate the digital world, paving the way for a future where users regain control over their digital lives. This vision of a decentralized Internet is not without its challenges, but its potential to reshape our digital interactions is undeniable, marking a significant step towards a more equitable and transparent digital age.

Blockchain & Cryptocurrencies

Web 3.0 harnesses the power of blockchain technology to redefine online interactions and transactions, laying the foundation for a digital ecosystem built on security and trust. At its core, this innovative framework facilitates transactions without the need for intermediaries, thanks to the immutable and transparent nature of blockchain.

Cryptocurrencies emerge as the new medium for financial exchanges, offering a decentralized alternative to traditional banking and payment systems. Moreover, smart contracts automate the execution of agreements, ensuring that terms are fulfilled without manual oversight. This shift towards trustless operations not only streamlines processes but also significantly enhances the reliability and efficiency of online transactions. In essence, Web 3.0 is setting the stage for a future where online interactions, whether financial or contractual, are conducted with unparalleled security, transparency, and without reliance on central authorities, embodying the true spirit of decentralization.

Semantic Web

The semantic web, a key pillar of Web 3.0, revolutionizes how data is utilized across the vast expanse of the Internet. It's not just about linking information; it is about understanding the context and nuances of words, enabling a smarter web that grasps the essence of user queries and interactions. This technology ensures that data isn't just accessible but is meaningfully connected across applications, businesses, and community borders, paving the way for a more intuitive and relevant user experience. By focusing on the semantics—the meaning and relationship of words—it dramatically enhances how content is discovered, shared, and presented, ensuring that what reaches the user is precisely what they need, when they need it. In essence, the semantic web propels us towards a future where the web is not only interconnected but intelligently aligned with the individual needs and contexts of its users, making information not just available but incredibly useful.

Artificial Intelligence & Machine Learning

Web 3.0 seamlessly integrates Artificial Intelligence (AI) and machine learning technologies to sift through and make sense of the burgeoning data produced by users across the digital landscape. This advanced analytical capability allows for the creation of highly customized and pertinent experiences for users, catering specifically to their preferences, behaviors, and interactions online. By employing sophisticated algorithms that learn and adapt over time, Web 3.0 can offer unprecedented levels of personalization, thereby revolutionizing the way users engage with content, services, and each other in the interconnected web of the future.

Interoperability

Web 3.0 is designed to transcend traditional barriers between different applications and devices, fostering an environment where users can effortlessly access and interact with their data regardless of their physical location or the device they're using. This vision of a seamlessly connected digital ecosystem allows for a fluid, intuitive user experience that aligns with the modern world's demands for flexibility and accessibility. By breaking down silos and enabling data to flow freely across platforms, Web 3.0 promises a future where the digital space is more integrated, user-centric, and adaptable to the ever-evolving needs of individuals navigating the online world.

Virtual, Augmented, Extended Reality

Let's explore the fascinating realm of XR—Extended Reality—a term that embraces the full spectrum of immersive technologies designed to augment our experience of the world. XR is an umbrella that shelters Virtual Reality (VR), Augmented Reality (AR), and Mixed Reality (MR), each offering unique ways to blend the digital and physical into experiences that are transforming how we interact, learn, and entertain ourselves in the Web3 landscape.

Virtual Reality (VR) takes you on a journey to a completely digital universe, disconnecting you from the physical world and immersing you in a virtual one. Imagine strapping on a VR headset and being transported to the surface of Mars, walking among dinosaurs, or standing in the Sistine Chapel—all from your living room. VR creates these immersive experiences by replacing your real-world environment with a digital one, where every turn of your head and movement of your hand is mirrored in a virtual space.

Augmented Reality (AR), on the other hand, enhances your real-world surroundings by overlaying digital information on top of it. It's like having a superpower that allows you to see information and virtual objects in your physical space. Picture pointing your smartphone at a historical monument and seeing its history pop up on your screen or watching a dinosaur roam your backyard through the lens of your tablet. AR adds depth and interaction to our perception of reality, making learning more engaging and everyday tasks more enriched.

Mixed Reality (MR) is where things get even more interesting, merging the best of both VR and AR. It creates a hybrid environment where physical and digital objects co-exist and interact in real time. Think of a surgeon practicing a complex procedure on a holographic patient or an engineer manipulating 3D models of machinery that appear to be right in front of them. MR is paving the way for collaborative, interactive experiences that could revolutionize industries by combining the immersive quality of VR with the interactive potential of AR.

The applications of XR are vast and varied, extending far beyond gaming and entertainment. In education, it is opening new ways of learning that are more interactive and impactful. In healthcare, it is providing innovative solutions for treatment and training. And in retail, it is changing how we shop, offering virtual try-ons and immersive explorations of products.

As we step further into the era of Web3, the potential of XR technologies to enhance our digital interactions is only just beginning to unfold. With each advancement in VR, AR, and MR, we're not just moving towards more immersive ways of experiencing the digital world; we're also looking at a future where the lines between the physical and virtual are increasingly blurred, creating endless possibilities for innovation, connection, and exploration. The journey into XR is a testament to human creativity and technological progress, inviting us to reimagine the fabric of our digital lives.

User Sovereignty

In the evolving landscape of Web 3.0, the concept of user sovereignty stands as a revolutionary pillar, heralding an era where users are empowered to control their digital presence. This new web phase is characterized not just by the decentralization of networks but by a significant shift in power dynamics, favoring individual autonomy over corporate monopolies. Here's a deeper view into the facets that enrich the narrative of user sovereignty in Web 3.0:

Interoperability and Cross-Platform Experiences: A key aspect of user sovereignty in Web 3.0 is its push towards interoperability, allowing seamless interactions across diverse digital platforms without compromising data control. This vision for a connected yet decentralized web promises a future where users can move freely across digital spaces, guided by a unified identity they own and control, breaking free from the silos of the current Internet.

Self-Sovereign Identity (SSI): Central to achieving user sovereignty is the adoption of self-sovereign identity systems. SSI hands users the keys to their digital identity, enabling control over personal data and online credentials without relying on central authorities. This autonomy reshapes online interactions, ensuring privacy and consent are at the forefront of digital transactions and communications.

Economic Empowerment Through Tokenization: Web 3.0's emphasis on user sovereignty introduces novel economic models powered by tokenization and cryptocurrencies. Users can now directly monetize their contributions and participation in the digital space—be it through creative endeavors, gaming, or active engagement in decentralized platforms. This not only democratizes the digital economy but also opens up new avenues for creators and participants to be compensated for their value creation.

Challenges and Considerations: Despite the optimistic vision, the journey towards full user sovereignty is fraught with challenges. Key among these is the need for enhanced digital literacy to navigate and secure digital assets effectively. Additionally, the potential for digital fragmentation and the quest for a regulatory balance that safeguards user rights without hampering innovation are critical considerations that need addressing as Web 3.0 evolves.

Community Governance and Participation: At the heart of Web 3.0's user sovereignty is a shift towards community-driven governance. Unlike the top-down decision-making paradigms of traditional platforms, Web 3.0 envisions a world where users, as stakeholders, actively participate in shaping the digital platforms and ecosystems they engage with. This collective approach to governance not only empowers users but also fosters a more inclusive and equitable digital world.

In sum, user sovereignty in Web 3.0 is not merely a feature; it is the foundation of a transformative digital era aimed at giving users unprecedented control over their online lives. By championing decentralization, interoperability, and economic empowerment, Web 3.0 sets the stage for a more open, secure, and user-centric Internet. However, realizing this vision requires navigating a complex landscape of technological, social, and regulatory challenges—a journey that promises to redefine our digital future.

⬡ Risk Management and Portfolio Diversification in Crypto Investing

Crypto may be exciting, but navigating its risks is crucial. Understanding potential pitfalls like price swings, regulation shifts, cyber threats, and illiquidity is key. To tackle these, assess the likelihood and impact of each risk before investing. Luckily, tools like diversification, stop-loss orders, and smart position sizing can help mitigate damage. Remember, education is your armor - stay informed about the evolving crypto landscape to stay ahead of the curve.

Principles of Risk Management in Cryptocurrency Investing

Navigating the rollercoaster world of cryptocurrency investing requires more than just a sturdy seatbelt; it demands a comprehensive risk management strategy tailored to the unique challenges and opportunities this market presents. Let's explore the nuances of managing risk in the crypto sphere, unraveling the complexities to safeguard your investments and maximize potential returns.

Understanding the Risks

First up, volatility is the name of the game in crypto. Prices can skyrocket or plummet faster than you can say "blockchain," influenced by everything from tweets to regulatory announcements. But the thrill of volatility isn't the only risk on the horizon. The ever-changing regulatory landscape can turn today's investment strategy on its head tomorrow, making it essential to stay informed and adaptable.

Then there's the digital Wild West of security threats. From hackers eyeing your digital gold to the pitfalls of human error—like sending funds to the wrong address—navigating security risks is paramount. And let's not forget about liquidity; being able to sell without moving the market is a luxury not afforded by all tokens.

Beyond the market itself, there's the risk of putting your trust in the wrong platform. Exchange insolvencies, wallet vulnerabilities, and the fine print in smart contracts can all pose significant risks. Moreover, the psychological rollercoaster of investing—chasing losses or getting swept up in the euphoria of gains—can lead to rash decisions if not kept in check.

Strategies to Shield Your Investments

Diversification is your first line of defense. Don't put all your eggs in one crypto basket. Spread your investments across different assets, sectors, and even outside of crypto to mitigate the impact of a single asset's downturn.

Make stop-loss and take-profit orders your best friends. These tools automatically sell assets at your predetermined price points, helping you lock in profits and cut losses without having to watch the market 24/7.

Be smart about how much you invest in each asset. Position sizing helps you avoid oversized losses by matching investment sizes with the risk level of each asset and your overall risk tolerance.

Regular portfolio reviews and rebalancing are like routine check-ups for your investments. They ensure your portfolio aligns with your risk appetite and investment goals, adjusting as needed to keep you on track.

Only invest what you can afford to lose. In the volatile world of crypto, safeguarding your financial well-being is crucial. This means using disposable income for investments, not funds earmarked for essentials.

Educate yourself continuously. That means constantly doing your own research. The crypto market is ever evolving, and staying informed about market trends, technological advancements, and regulatory changes can help you navigate risks more effectively.

Risk management in cryptocurrency investing isn't about avoiding losses; it is about making informed, strategic decisions that align with your financial goals and risk tolerance. By understanding the multifaceted risks and employing a range of strategies to mitigate them, you can position yourself to navigate the crypto market's volatility with confidence.

Remember, in the world of cryptocurrency, knowledge, and preparation are your most valuable assets.

Portfolio Diversification in Cryptocurrency Investing

Embarking on the journey of cryptocurrency investing is much like navigating the vast expanse of the open sea, where the waters are as unpredictable as they are enticing. The secret to maintaining your course through these turbulent waves? Diversification. It's your financial compass, ensuring you're not overly reliant on a single wind to propel you forward. Imagine you're at a bustling market that spans the globe, with stalls brimming with an array of goods from every corner of the earth. It wouldn't be wise to spend all your resources in one place when there's so much more to explore and gain from.

Diversification in the crypto market means spreading your investments across a variety of assets. It's not just about choosing between Bitcoin and Ethereum; it is about venturing into the burgeoning sectors of DeFi, NFTs, and even taking calculated risks on emerging small cap cryptos. This approach is about minimizing risks while maximizing exposure to potential opportunities in a fast-evolving landscape.

But why stop at crypto? The investment universe is vast, encompassing traditional assets such as stocks, bonds, and real estate, which can add layers of stability and risk mitigation to your portfolio. Adding stablecoins to the mix can act as a buffer against crypto market volatility, allowing you to pause and strategize without fully retreating from the market dynamics.

For those with a taste for adventure and a tolerance for higher risks, the frontiers of ICOs and venture capital investments in blockchain startups beckon. While these paths are fraught with uncertainty, they also hold the promise of groundbreaking returns, akin to discovering uncharted territories rich with potential.

Effective diversification is akin to weaving a robust tapestry from various threads—each representing different sectors, asset classes, and opportunities. This strategic blend not only guards against the storms of market volatility but also positions you to capture the winds of growth and innovation. As you traverse the ever-expanding crypto ecosystem, let diversification be the guiding principle that shapes your investment journey. This approach, grounded in balance, exploration, and informed decision-making, paves the way for a resilient and dynamic portfolio. In embracing the full spectrum of investing possibilities, you chart a course toward a future where your financial portfolio is not just diversified, but also reflective of the rich, multifaceted world of digital and traditional assets. It's a journey that promises not just financial returns, but also a deeper understanding and engagement with the transformative power of blockchain technology and beyond.

Integrating Cryptos into a Broader Portfolio

Venturing into the realm of cryptocurrencies as part of a traditional investment portfolio is akin to navigating the frontier of a new financial paradigm. It's an acknowledgment of the burgeoning potential of digital assets, poised to complement the stalwarts of investment portfolios—stocks, bonds, and real estate. Yet, integrating these digital pioneers into your financial strategy isn't a simple addition; it is a nuanced recalibration that demands a keen understanding of your financial landscape and an appetite for exploration.

Firstly, consider how these digital assets fit into the tapestry of your financial goals and risk appetite. Cryptocurrencies, with their notorious volatility, are not for the faint-hearted. They are the high seas of the investment world—capable of towering highs and profound lows. Allocating a portion of your portfolio to cryptocurrencies should mirror your readiness for turbulence, with a sliver of your investments dedicated to these digital assets, recognizing them as both high-risk and potentially high-reward ventures.

The volatility of cryptocurrencies is a double-edged sword. On one hand, it presents the tantalizing prospect of significant gains; on the other, it challenges your portfolio's equilibrium. Navigating this requires not just a sturdy financial keel but also the wisdom to know your own financial seasickness tolerance. It's about ensuring that the waves of crypto volatility don't capsize your long-term investment journey.

Liquidity also varies widely across the crypto spectrum. While titans like Bitcoin and Ethereum boast substantial liquidity, venturing into the less charted waters of smaller altcoins can sometimes leave investors stranded in a market downturn. It's crucial, then, to understand the liquidity landscape of these assets, ensuring you're not left adrift when you wish to dock your investments elsewhere.

Regulatory winds and the security of digital assets also chart the course for crypto inclusion in your portfolio. The regulatory horizon is ever-changing, with potential storms and safe harbors emerging as governments and institutions respond to the crypto evolution. Protecting your digital treasure from the modern-day pirates of hacking and fraud means arming yourself with the digital equivalents of locks, vaults, and maps—hardware wallets, secure exchanges, and a vigilant eye on your assets.

Diversifying within the crypto realm offers a buffer against the volatility and uncertainty of individual assets. Imagine a fleet of ships each exploring different routes—some may face storms, but others will discover new lands. Similarly, mixing established cryptos with promising new ventures can balance risk and reward. Hedging strategies and a long-term view anchor this approach, allowing investors to weather short-term fluctuations with an eye on the horizon of technological advancement and market maturation.

Embarking on this journey requires not just a map but a commitment to continual learning and adaptation. The crypto world is in constant flux, with new developments, technologies, and opportunities emerging at a rapid clip. Staying informed is not just beneficial; it is essential for navigating these waters successfully.

Incorporating cryptocurrencies into your investment portfolio is a voyage into uncharted financial waters. It's a balance of harnessing the innovative potential of these digital assets while navigating their volatility with prudence and informed strategy. Like any great exploration, it holds the promise of rich rewards for those who navigate it wisely, armed with knowledge, strategy, and an adventurous spirit. This integration marks a bold step toward a future where digital and traditional assets coalesce, offering a new vista of investment possibilities.

Decentralized Finance

Decentralized Finance, or DeFi, is revolutionizing the way we think about financial services by eliminating the need for traditional financial intermediaries like banks, brokerages, and exchanges. Built primarily on the Ethereum blockchain, DeFi uses smart contracts to facilitate various financial transactions directly between parties. This emerging financial landscape is defined by its permissionless nature, allowing anyone with an Internet connection to participate, and its transparency, with all transactions and smart contract operations visible and verifiable by anyone.

The essence of DeFi lies in its ability to make financial services more accessible, inclusive, and efficient. It encompasses a wide array of services, including lending and borrowing platforms that enable users to lend or borrow funds directly from each other, decentralized exchanges (DEXs) that allow for direct cryptocurrency trades without a central authority, and platforms that offer yield farming and liquidity mining opportunities for cryptocurrency holders to earn rewards. DeFi also introduces the concept of synthetic assets, which represent other assets like fiat currencies or stocks in the form of ERC-20 tokens, allowing for exposure to a wide range of assets without physically holding them.

One of the key features of DeFi is the use of stablecoins, cryptocurrencies designed to minimize volatility by pegging their value to stable assets such as fiat currencies. This integration of stablecoins into DeFi platforms provides a stable medium of exchange and value, essential for the smooth operation of financial services on the blockchain.

Despite its numerous benefits, DeFi is not without challenges and risks. The sector is known for its high volatility and is susceptible to security vulnerabilities in the code for smart contracts, which can lead to significant financial losses. Furthermore, the regulatory environment surrounding DeFi is still evolving, posing potential risks for users and platforms alike. Additionally, issues of scalability and efficiency remain as the DeFi ecosystem continues to grow and attract more users.

In summary, Decentralized Finance represents a significant shift towards a more open, transparent, and user-controlled financial system. It democratizes access to financial services, enabling innovation and efficiency beyond traditional financial models. However, navigating this new landscape requires caution, as the DeFi space is complex, rapidly evolving, and fraught with risks that investors must carefully consider.

Decentralized Physical Infrastructure Networks (DPINs)

Decentralized Physical Infrastructure Networks (DPINs) represent a pioneering shift towards embedding the ethos of decentralization into the fabric of our physical world, particularly in how we manage and interact with essential infrastructure like energy grids, water systems, telecommunications, and transportation networks. The vision behind DPINs is to transform these critical systems to become more resilient, efficient, and attuned to the needs of the communities they serve.

At the core of DPINs is the move away from traditional centralized models, where decision-making and operational control are vested in a singular authority, towards a distributed framework. This fundamental shift promises enhanced system resilience by eliminating single points of failure and fostering flexibility in operations. It allows for peer-to-peer interactions, cutting out the intermediaries and fostering direct connections between users and providers. This could lead to streamlined processes, reduced costs, and a more personalized approach to service delivery.

A particularly exciting aspect of DPINs is the potential application of blockchain technology and smart contracts. These digital tools can automate administrative tasks, secure transactions, and foster a transparent, trust-based environment among all participants. This digital backbone, combined with decentralized control, hands back significant power to local communities. It allows for a more customized, responsive approach to managing resources, potentially revolutionizing everything from how we consume energy to how we access clean water.

The sustainability angle of DPINs cannot be overstated. By promoting localized control and optimizing resource distribution, these networks could significantly reduce waste and support the shift towards renewable energy sources. Imagine community-based solar projects or microgrids that not only reduce carbon footprints but also empower local economies.

The benefits of such a system are manifold. From increasing the resilience of our infrastructure to fostering innovation through broad stakeholder participation, DPINs could redefine service delivery to be more coordinated with local needs and preferences. Moreover, by supporting the transition to greener, more sustainable energy sources, DPINs align closely with global sustainability goals. They also hold the promise of economic and social empowerment, particularly for underserved communities, by enabling local ownership and decision-making.

However, the road to realizing the full potential of DPINs is fraught with challenges, from technological barriers and regulatory complexities to financial sustainability questions. Overcoming these obstacles will require a concerted effort to develop robust governance frameworks, establish technical standards, and foster a culture of active engagement among all stakeholders.

DPINs offer a tantalizing glimpse into a future where our physical infrastructure systems are not only smarter and more sustainable but also more democratic and equitable. As this concept continues to develop, it holds the promise of realigning our critical services with the values of sustainability, equity, and communal empowerment, charting a course towards a more resilient and responsive physical world.

Tokenization

Tokenization is revolutionizing the way we think about asset ownership and investment in the blockchain era. It's a process that turns the rights to any asset—be it a piece of art, a slice of real estate, or a vintage car—into a digital token on a blockchain. This isn't just about making transactions digital; it is about opening up a world of opportunities for assets that were previously out of reach for many due to prohibitive costs or market barriers.

At its heart, tokenization breaks down assets into smaller, more affordable pieces. Imagine owning a fraction of a Picasso painting or a piece of a skyscraper in downtown Manhattan. This concept, known as fractional ownership, isn't entirely new, but blockchain technology brings it to a whole new level by enhancing accessibility, liquidity, and security.

One of the most compelling aspects of tokenization is its ability to breathe liquidity into markets that were traditionally considered illiquid. Real estate, for instance, is notorious for its long, cumbersome sales process, but tokenization allows these assets to be traded much like stocks on an exchange. This not only makes buying and selling easier but also opens these investment opportunities to a global audience.

Security and transparency are other hallmarks of tokenization. Since transactions are recorded on a blockchain, they benefit from the technology's inherent characteristics: immutability, decentralization, and transparency. This means that once a transaction is made, it can't be altered or deleted, providing a clear, tamper-proof record of ownership and transaction history.

The range of assets that can be tokenized is vast and varied. From tangible assets like real estate and art to intangible ones like securities, commodities, and even intellectual property rights, the potential for tokenization is nearly limitless. This could fundamentally change how we invest in and profit from various assets, making investment opportunities more democratic and accessible to a broader range of people.

Despite its vast potential, tokenization isn't without its challenges. The regulatory landscape, for instance, is still a work in progress, with many jurisdictions figuring out how to categorize and regulate digital tokens. There's also the need for standardization across platforms to ensure that tokens representing the same asset are interchangeable, and concerns about cybersecurity and fraud remain paramount.

In conclusion, tokenization is poised to redefine the principles of asset ownership, making it more inclusive, efficient, and secure. It offers a glimpse into a future where investment opportunities are no longer gated by wealth or geography but are accessible to anyone with an Internet connection. As the technology and regulatory frameworks evolve, tokenization could very well become the backbone of a new, more open financial system.

⬡ Investment Analysis Framework for Cryptocurrencies

Investing in the whirlwind world of cryptocurrencies isn't for the faint-hearted. It's a realm where the dizzying volatility can turn fortunes on a dime, making a well-rounded investment analysis framework not just beneficial but essential for anyone looking to invest in the Cryptoverse. This approach to cryptocurrency investment analysis is multifaceted, blending an understanding of broader market trends, a deep analysis into the nuts and bolts of individual projects, and the savvy application of technical indicators to paint a comprehensive picture of potential investment opportunities.

First up, let's talk about market trends. The cryptocurrency landscape doesn't exist in a vacuum; it is at the mercy of global economic shifts, regulatory winds, and breakthroughs in technology, all of which can send ripples across the market. Keeping a pulse on these macro trends can give investors a heads-up on where the market's headed, offering clues on when to hold tight and when it might be time to make a move. Equally telling is the adoption rate of a cryptocurrency. Are businesses warming up to it? Is it gaining traction among users? A "yes" could signal a growing confidence in the asset, hinting at an upward trajectory for both demand and price.

Digging deeper, the project's fundamentals come under the microscope. What problem is cryptocurrency trying to solve? Is it just another me-too project, or does it bring something groundbreaking to the table? A project with a clear, innovative use case that taps into real-world needs is often more poised for longevity and value. The brains behind the operation matter too. A project spearheaded by a seasoned, transparent team stands a better chance of navigating the choppy waters of the crypto world. Don't overlook the community either; a passionate, engaged user base can be a cryptocurrency's best advocate, signaling a project's credibility and long-term viability.

Then there's the fine art of technical analysis. By charting the asset's price history, investors can spot trends, key resistance and support levels, and patterns that might hint at future price movements. Volume analysis and momentum indicators like the Relative Strength Index (RSI) and Moving Average Convergence Divergence (MACD) can offer additional insights, flagging potential market entry or exit points.

But it is not just about spotting the green flags; a savvy investor keeps an eye out for potential risks too. From regulatory hurdles to market competition and the ever-present specter of volatility, understanding the risks is key to navigating the investment landscape. And don't forget the value of cross-analysis—comparing a project against its peers can unearth gems that stand out from the crowd.

In summary, a solid investment analysis framework for cryptocurrencies isn't just a nice-to-have; it is your compass in the unpredictable world of digital assets. By marrying market insights with a keen evaluation of project fundamentals and technical cues, investors can chart a course through the crypto market with greater confidence, poised to capitalize on opportunities while keeping an eye on the risks. It's a dynamic balancing act, but one that's crucial for anyone looking to tap into the potential of cryptocurrency investments.

⬡ Banks vs. Cryptocurrency Exchanges

We often find ourselves toggling between the familiar, time-honored institutions of banks and the burgeoning sphere of cryptocurrency exchanges. At a glance, these entities might seem to operate on entirely different wavelengths, yet, when we peel back the layers, their core functions reveal some striking parallels alongside their distinct divergences.

Banks have long stood as the pillars of financial stability, guardians of our savings, facilitators of our transactions, and advisors on our financial journeys. They're the traditional powerhouses where deposits are made, loans are sourced, and financial assets are safeguarded. Banks operate within a heavily regulated framework, ensuring a degree of security and trust for their clientele, albeit often at the cost of slower transaction times and layers of fees.

On the flip side of the coin, cryptocurrency exchanges have emerged as the digital age's answer to asset trading and management, serving as bustling marketplaces for buying, selling, and holding a vast array of digital currencies. Much like banks, they provide the infrastructure for financial transactions, but with a twist — they cater to a digital-first audience with an appetite for the decentralized, borderless, and often more rapid movement of assets that cryptocurrencies offer.

Centralized exchanges, or CEXs, mirror the traditional banking model in several ways, acting as intermediaries that oversee transactions. They bring a user-friendly interface to the table, often simplifying the complex world of crypto trading for newcomers and seasoned traders alike. These platforms usually emphasize regulatory compliance, including know-your-customer (KYC) and anti-money laundering (AML) protocols, much like banks, to foster a secure trading environment. However, this centralization also means users entrust their digital assets to the exchange, similar to depositing money in a bank, which has both its conveniences and vulnerabilities.

Decentralized exchanges, or DEXs, challenge the traditional model by removing the middleman from the equation. They facilitate direct peer-to-peer transactions through smart contracts on the blockchain, championing the ethos of decentralization that is core to cryptocurrency's appeal. Here, users retain control over their private keys — akin to holding onto their cash or valuables, but without a centralized authority to turn to if things go awry. This model emphasizes privacy and autonomy, though it also demands a higher degree of personal responsibility and technical know-how from its users.

The choice between engaging with a bank, a CEX, or a DEX comes down to a trade-off between the security and convenience offered by centralized institutions and the freedom, responsibility, and sometimes the risk associated with navigating the decentralized landscape. As we traverse this evolving financial terrain, understanding these platforms' foundational workings — recognizing their strengths, their limitations, and the unique value propositions they offer — becomes crucial. This knowledge empowers us to make informed decisions that align with our financial goals, risk tolerance, and the degree of control we wish to exercise over our assets. In the grand scheme of things, whether it's through a bank, a CEX, or a DEX, the journey towards financial empowerment and literacy continues, reshaping our interactions with money in profound and exciting ways.

⬡ From Plastic to Digital: The Evolution of Payment Systems and the Rise of Cryptocurrency

The journey of credit cards, from their inception to widespread adoption, mirrors in many ways the evolutionary path of cryptocurrencies, offering valuable insights into how new financial technologies gain acceptance and transform economic landscapes.

The credit card's story began in 1950 with the Diners Club card, the first multi-purpose charge card, an innovation that initially catered to a niche market of travelers and entertainment enthusiasts. This novel concept allowed users to purchase goods and services on credit, with the promise of later repayment, introducing a new level of convenience and flexibility in personal finance. The adoption of credit cards underwent several phases, evolving from a novelty to a necessity. Early adoption was driven by the allure of convenience and the exclusivity associated with card membership. However, widespread usage required overcoming significant hurdles: establishing trust among consumers, building a network of merchants willing to accept cards, and creating a robust infrastructure for processing transactions.

Similarly, cryptocurrencies embarked on their journey in 2009 with the introduction of Bitcoin. Like the early days of credit cards, initial crypto adoption was limited, appealing mainly to tech enthusiasts and visionaries attracted by its decentralized nature and the potential for peer-to-peer transactions without intermediaries. The path to mainstream acceptance for cryptocurrencies has been marked by challenges, including regulatory scrutiny, volatility concerns, and the need for user-friendly exchanges and wallets.

Both credit cards and cryptocurrencies have had to navigate the delicate balance of innovation and regulation. For credit cards, regulatory frameworks evolved to protect consumers and standardize practices, paving the way for global acceptance and integration into the financial system. Cryptocurrencies, while still in the midst of navigating regulatory landscapes, are seeing increased institutional interest and integration into traditional financial services, signaling a shift towards broader acceptance.

The adoption of credit cards transformed how people borrow, spend, and manage money, embedding plastic into the fabric of global commerce. Cryptocurrencies, in a parallel narrative, are gradually reshaping notions of money, value, and transactional freedom. Both movements reflect a broader theme of technological advancement in finance, where initial skepticism and regulatory challenges give way to innovation, leading to new forms of payment and financial interaction.

In comparing the adoption of credit cards with that of cryptocurrencies, it becomes apparent that groundbreaking financial technologies often follow a trajectory from skepticism to niche acceptance and eventually, widespread use. Each phase of adoption is propelled by a combination of technological advancements, regulatory clarity, and shifts in consumer behavior, ultimately leading to a redefined financial landscape. As cryptocurrencies continue to mature, they may mirror the credit card's journey, moving from novelty to an integral part of financial systems worldwide.

The pace at which cryptocurrencies are gaining acceptance is notably faster than the gradual path credit cards took to become a staple of financial transactions. This accelerated adoption can be attributed to the digital era we live in, where technology rapidly evolves and integrates into daily life at an unprecedented speed. The internet has provided a fertile ground for cryptocurrencies to grow, with information spreading quickly and communities forming around blockchain projects worldwide. Additionally, the global nature of cryptocurrencies, transcending borders and offering decentralized transactions, appeals to a digitally savvy generation eager for financial autonomy and innovation. This fast-paced adoption is further fueled by the increasing involvement of institutional investors and the integration of blockchain technology into mainstream financial services.

Adding to the narrative of cryptocurrency adoption is the potential for a shift towards more prudent financial habits. Unlike credit cards, which often encourage spending money one doesn't have through revolving credit and minimum payments, cryptocurrencies can inspire a return to living within one's means. The use of cryptocurrencies requires upfront ownership of assets, meaning individuals must possess the digital currency before they can transact. This model promotes a sense of financial responsibility and planning, as users become more mindful of their spending, investment choices, and the importance of saving. In a world where debt has become a widespread concern, the inherent characteristics of cryptocurrencies offer a blueprint for a financial system that encourages sustainability and accountability.

This paradigm shift towards faster adoption and a potentially more responsible financial ethos underscores the transformative power of cryptocurrencies. As digital currencies continue to evolve and gain acceptance, they not only challenge the traditional banking and financial systems but also offer a chance to redefine personal finance. The speed of crypto adoption, coupled with its capacity to encourage living within one's means, highlights the revolutionary potential of blockchain technology to influence not just how transactions are made, but also how individuals and societies approach the concept of money and financial health in the digital age.

⬡ About Exchanges

Let's unwrap the workings of cryptocurrency exchanges, the bustling hubs where digital currencies like Bitcoin and Ethereum change hands. These platforms are where the magic of trading happens, allowing users to buy, sell, and trade cryptocurrencies. Whether you're a seasoned trader or just starting, getting a handle on the basics of how exchanges operate is key to navigating the crypto waters smoothly.

When you first step into the world of cryptocurrency trading, you'll start by setting up an account on an exchange. If you're using a centralized platform, you'll likely go through a verification process to meet regulatory requirements, much like opening a bank account. On the flip side, decentralized exchanges often skip this step, offering a different kind of entry point into the market.

Once you're in, you'll need to fund your account. On centralized exchanges, you might deposit traditional fiat currency through various payment methods. If you're diving into decentralized platforms or prefer using crypto, you'll transfer digital assets from your wallet to the exchange.

Here's where the trading action begins. You have options like buy and sell orders, where you can specify the price you are willing to trade at. There are market orders that execute instantly at the current price and limit orders that wait for the market to hit your target price. Exchanges also offer advanced trading features, such as leveraging your position or setting up futures contracts and stop-loss orders to hedge against market volatility.

Understanding the concepts of liquidity, order books, and trading pairs is like getting a peek behind the curtain of the trading stage. Liquidity is all about how easily you can execute trades without impacting the market price too much. A liquid market is bustling, with lots of buyers and sellers making trades flow smoothly.

The order book is your window into the market's soul, showing live buy and sell orders for a particular crypto pair. It's a dynamic list that offers insights into potential price movements, letting you see where the demand is stacking up.

Speaking of pairs, trading pairs are the bread and butter of crypto trading. They pair up two currencies, like BTC/USD, allowing you to trade one for the other. Exchanges host a variety of these pairs, giving traders the flexibility to pivot between different strategies and markets.

All these elements come together to make cryptocurrency exchanges the vibrant marketplaces they are, offering a platform for the fast-paced world of crypto trading. Whether you're looking to make quick trades or invest long-term, understanding how exchanges work is fundamental to your journey in the cryptocurrency universe. It's about making informed decisions and steering through the exciting yet complex landscape of digital currency trading.

Centralized Exchanges

Centralized exchanges, often referred to as CEXs, are akin to traditional stock exchanges but for the digital age, acting as the beating heart of the cryptocurrency trading world. These platforms are where the vast majority of crypto transactions take place, offering a bridge between the traditional financial world and the burgeoning realm of digital currencies.

At their core, CEXs operate under the watchful eye of a central authority — the company that runs the exchange. This setup allows for a range of user-friendly features that make these platforms particularly appealing to both crypto newcomers and seasoned traders. For starters, they offer straightforward interfaces that simplify the often complex world of cryptocurrency trading. Whether you're looking to make a quick purchase of Bitcoin, trade some Ethereum, or explore the depths of altcoins, CEXs provide a comprehensive and accessible gateway.

One of the standout benefits of centralized exchanges is their high liquidity. Thanks to their large user bases, these platforms ensure that trades can be executed swiftly and at prices close to the market rate. This liquidity is crucial during volatile market conditions, allowing traders to enter and exit positions without significantly affecting the price of the asset.

Security and regulatory compliance are other pillars of the CEX experience. In an environment as wild and unpredictable as the crypto market, having a regulated platform can offer a sense of security. Centralized exchanges adhere to strict regulatory standards, including Know Your Customer (KYC) and Anti-Money Laundering (AML) protocols. While this means users must share personal information to access the full suite of services, it also adds a layer of protection against fraud and money laundering.

But it's not all smooth sailing. The centralized nature of these exchanges means that users' assets are held by the platform, which has historically been a magnet for hackers. High-profile breaches have led to significant losses, underscoring the importance of robust security measures. In response, leading exchanges have bolstered their defenses, implementing advanced security protocols and offering insurance to protect users' funds.

Moreover, CEXs are more than just places to trade. They often serve as a one-stop-shop for crypto enthusiasts, providing a variety of services including fiat on-ramps and off-ramps, staking, savings accounts, and even educational resources to help users navigate the crypto ecosystem.

In sum, centralized exchanges play a crucial role in the crypto landscape, offering ease of use, high liquidity, and a regulated environment for trading digital assets. While they may carry certain risks related to security and privacy, the leading platforms are continuously evolving, adopting innovative technologies and protocols to enhance user experience and safety. As the bridge between traditional finance and the future of money, CEXs are indispensable for anyone looking to explore the world of cryptocurrency.

Decentralized Exchanges

Decentralized exchanges, or DEXs, represent a transformative approach to trading cryptocurrencies, embodying the core principles of decentralization that are fundamental to the blockchain ethos. Unlike their centralized counterparts, DEXs operate without a central authority, facilitating direct transactions between users through an automated process known as smart contracts. This innovative model offers a unique set of advantages and challenges, reshaping the landscape of cryptocurrency trading.

At the heart of decentralized exchanges is the principle of self-custody. Users of DEXs retain control over their private keys and, consequently, their assets. This direct control mitigates the risks associated with centralized platforms, where assets stored on the exchange are vulnerable to hacks and other security breaches. The emphasis on self-custody aligns with the decentralized nature of blockchain technology, offering users full sovereignty over their funds.

One of the standout features of DEXs is the enhanced privacy they offer. Since transactions are executed directly between users' wallets without the need for intermediaries, personal information is not required to trade. This anonymity is a significant draw for those who value privacy and wish to operate within the cryptocurrency space without revealing their identity.

However, the decentralized structure of DEXs comes with its own set of challenges, particularly regarding liquidity. Unlike centralized exchanges, which can leverage their large user base to ensure a high volume of trades, DEXs often struggle with lower liquidity. This can result in slippage—a difference between the expected price of a trade and the price at which the trade is executed—especially for large orders or less popular tokens. To address this, some DEXs have introduced liquidity pools and incentivization mechanisms to encourage users to supply liquidity, thereby enhancing trade efficiency.

Interoperability is another hallmark of decentralized exchanges, allowing them to support a wide array of tokens and assets across different blockchain networks. This openness fosters a diverse trading environment where users can access a broad spectrum of digital assets. Moreover, the smart contract framework enables not just trading but also complex financial operations like staking, lending, and yield farming, further expanding the utility of DEXs within the DeFi ecosystem.

Despite these advantages, the user experience on DEXs can be more complex than on centralized platforms. Navigating smart contracts, understanding liquidity provisions, and managing wallet security require a higher level of technical knowledge. This complexity can be a barrier to entry for newcomers to the cryptocurrency space. Additionally, the lack of regulatory oversight in decentralized environments raises questions about compliance and the potential for illicit activities, though this is an area of ongoing development and debate within the community.

In essence, decentralized exchanges offer a vision of what a fully autonomous and decentralized financial system might look like. They champion user autonomy, privacy, and access to a diverse range of assets without the need for traditional financial intermediaries. As the technology and infrastructure surrounding DEXs continue to evolve, they are likely to play an increasingly vital role in the cryptocurrency market, offering users a more transparent, secure, and inclusive way to trade and engage with digital assets.

Security and Regulation

In the bustling world of cryptocurrency exchanges, the twin pillars of security and regulation stand at the forefront, safeguarding the vast digital fortunes that flow through these platforms daily. As these exchanges become the focal points for both seasoned investors and newcomers eager to wade into the crypto waters, their commitment to robust security measures and compliance with a kaleidoscope of global regulations becomes paramount.

At the heart of any exchange's defense strategy, you'll find a suite of security measures designed to fortify its digital battlements. Two-factor authentication (2FA) acts as the first line of defense, a simple yet effective way to ensure that access to an account requires more than just the correct password. Then there's cold storage, the digital equivalent of a high-security vault, where the bulk of an exchange's assets are kept offline, far from the clutches of would-be cyber thieves.

But the armory doesn't end there. Encryption and secure socket layer (SSL) protocols weave a protective cloak around data as it travels across the internet, shielding transaction details and personal information from prying eyes. And let's not forget the regular security audits— meticulous sweeps through an exchange's infrastructure conducted by eagle-eyed experts, hunting for vulnerabilities before malicious actors can exploit them.

Yet, despite these defenses, risks loom large. Phishing attacks that lure unsuspecting users, sophisticated hacks that breach exchange defenses, and the specter of internal fraud all pose significant threats. The loss of private keys — the cryptographically secure codes that unlock access to cryptocurrency holdings — can spell disaster, underscoring the critical importance of secure key management practices.

The regulatory landscape for cryptocurrency exchanges is a patchwork of global standards, with regulations varying dramatically from one jurisdiction to the next. Some countries have welcomed exchanges with open arms, establishing clear rules and licensing requirements that weave them into the broader financial tapestry while safeguarding investors. Others tread a more cautious path, casting a shadow of ambiguity or outright restriction that can stifle an exchange's operations within their borders.

Key regulatory hurdles include stringent anti-money laundering (AML) and know-your-customer (KYC) protocols designed to prevent cryptocurrencies from becoming conduits for illicit activities. The classification of certain tokens as securities brings additional layers of oversight, while data protection laws ensure that exchanges handle user information with the utmost care.

The dance between regulation and innovation is delicate. On one hand, stringent or unclear regulations can constrict the industry's growth, potentially pushing the boundaries of crypto innovation toward more welcoming shores. On the other hand, a well-defined regulatory framework can bolster the ecosystem, fostering a secure environment that encourages wider adoption and integration into the financial mainstream.

As cryptocurrency exchanges navigate this complex web of security challenges and regulatory requirements, their role in the broader acceptance and growth of digital assets becomes ever more critical. By championing rigorous security practices and aligning with regulatory standards, these platforms not only protect their users but also lay the groundwork for a future where cryptocurrencies hold a revered place in the global financial system.

⬡ Wallets

A cryptocurrency wallet is a digital tool, physical medium, program, or service that stores the public and/or private keys for cryptocurrency transactions. In addition to this basic function of storing keys, a cryptocurrency wallet more often offers the functionality of encrypting and/or signing information. Signing can for example result in executing a smart contract, a cryptocurrency transaction, identification, or legally signing a 'document'.

Cryptocurrency wallets are essential for users to send and receive digital currencies and monitor their balance. Wallets can be divided into several categories based on their functionality and how they store these keys:

Software Wallets: These wallets are applications that you can download to your computer or mobile device. They include:

Desktop Wallets: Installed on a personal computer, offering full control over the assets and keys.

Mobile Wallets: Apps on a smartphone, convenient for paying in physical stores by scanning QR codes.

Web Wallets: Accessed through Internet browsers, stored on a server controlled by a third party, and are convenient for quick transactions but less secure due to the risk of online theft.

Hardware Wallets: Physical devices designed to securely store cryptocurrency keys offline. They are considered one of the safest options because they are immune to online hacking attacks and can be used to sign transactions without exposing the keys to a potentially compromised computer.

Paper Wallets: Physical documents that contain a public address for receiving cryptocurrencies and a private key, which allows you to spend or transfer cryptocurrencies stored in that address. Paper wallets are a form of cold storage, meaning they are stored offline and are considered a secure way to hold cryptocurrency, albeit less convenient for quick transactions.

Security: The main priority, with various wallets offering various levels of security (e.g., two-factor authentication, multi-signature transactions).

Control: Some wallets give you full control over your keys and funds, while others may retain some control (especially custodial web wallets).

Transparency: Many wallets are open source, allowing users to review the code that controls the wallet.

Anonymity: While transactions are recorded on a public ledger, the identity of users can remain anonymous, depending on the wallet's privacy features.

Compatibility: Certain wallets support a wide range of cryptocurrencies, while others are designed for a specific blockchain.

It's crucial for users to understand the responsibilities that come with managing a cryptocurrency wallet, including safeguarding their private keys and backup phrases to prevent loss of funds due to theft, device failure, or other mishaps.

Custodial Wallets

Custodial wallets reveal a landscape where simplicity and convenience intersect with the innovative realm of cryptocurrency. Custodial wallets are akin to a trusted intermediary in the traditional banking world but set within the dynamic and decentralized blockchain network. Here, the responsibility of managing the cryptographic keys that unlock access to cryptocurrency holdings is entrusted to a third party, such as a cryptocurrency exchange or a specialized wallet service. This delegation of responsibility brings with it a suite of features tailored to enhance the user experience, particularly for those new to the digital currency space.

One of the standout attractions of custodial wallets is their user-friendly nature, designed to lower the barrier to entry for engaging with cryptocurrencies. They streamline the complexities of blockchain transactions, offering a hands-off approach to key management that can appeal to beginners and those seeking convenience. The integration of custodial wallets with broader cryptocurrency services, such as trading platforms or interest-bearing accounts, further cements their role as a gateway to the ecosystem, providing a seamless transition between different services under a single umbrella.

However, the trade-off for this convenience is a shift in the locus of control and security. Placing trust in a third party to safeguard your digital assets introduces a level of vulnerability, underscored by historical instances of security breaches that have led to significant losses. The reliance on custodial services also brings into focus concerns around privacy, as the process of identity verification for Know Your Customer (KYC) compliance reduces the anonymity that is a hallmark of blockchain transactions. Moreover, the control exercised by custodians over user funds—manifested through potential account freezes, withdrawal limits, or service downtimes—highlights a departure from the self-sovereignty that defines the ethos of cryptocurrency ownership.

Non-Custodial Wallets

In contrast to the custodial model, non-custodial wallets place the power and responsibility of key management firmly in the hands of the user. This self-custody model resonates with the foundational principles of blockchain technology, offering an unmediated relationship with one's digital assets. It underscores a commitment to personal security practices and the autonomy to act without third-party intervention, albeit with the caveat that losing access to one's private keys or recovery phrases can lead to irreversible loss of assets.

The choice between custodial and non-custodial wallets embodies a broader decision about the values and priorities of cryptocurrency users. Those drawn to the convenience, integrated services, and recovery options of custodial wallets might be willing to navigate the associated risks and trade-offs. Conversely, individuals who value autonomy, privacy, and direct control over their digital assets may gravitate towards the non-custodial approach, embracing the responsibilities that come with it.

This exploration into custodial wallets not only highlights their role within the cryptocurrency ecosystem but also reflects the diverse needs and preferences of its participants. As the blockchain space continues to evolve, the dialogue between convenience and control, security and autonomy remains a central theme in the journey towards a more inclusive and accessible digital economy.

What Distinguishes Non-Custodial Wallets?

Imagine stepping into a realm where you reign supreme over your financial assets, free from the oversight of intermediaries. This is the promise of non-custodial wallets, which stand at the forefront of the cryptocurrency movement's push towards decentralization. They embody the principle of self-sovereignty, granting you unparalleled control and privacy over your digital treasures. In this landscape, your assets are secured by the might of your own practices, akin to a personal Fort Knox, but with a twist—the security of your holdings hinges on your vigilance in safeguarding your private keys.

The concept of a backup lifeline, through a recovery phrase, introduces a safety net into this ecosystem. It's akin to possessing a magical incantation that can summon your digital wealth on another device, should the original be lost or compromised. This feature highlights a balance between autonomy and security, providing a way to reclaim access to your assets across the vast expanse of the digital realm.

Navigating the Freedoms Offered by Non-Custodial Wallets

With the autonomy of non-custodial wallets comes a significant responsibility—the safeguarding of your private keys and recovery phrase. This duty is the bedrock of your digital independence, requiring a disciplined and meticulous approach to security. The liberty to manage your assets without intermediaries also demands a foundational understanding of cryptocurrency operations and security. This knowledge not only empowers effective wallet management but also fortifies defenses against potential threats.

Ease of use in non-custodial wallets has seen remarkable advancements, aiming to bridge the gap between complex security protocols and user-friendly interfaces. However, the journey from a novice user to a proficient one is filled with learning. Engaging with these wallets means embarking on a continuous journey of education, enhancing your understanding of the blockchain space, and refining your approach to digital asset management.

The privacy perks of non-custodial wallets offer a layer of anonymity in transactions, a feature increasingly coveted in an era where data privacy concerns loom large. By facilitating transactions without tying your identity directly to your wallet's activities, they provide a sanctuary for your digital interactions, free from the prying eyes of the digital world.

In essence, non-custodial wallets are not merely tools for engaging with the blockchain; they are a declaration of independence in the digital age. They represent a commitment to the principles of decentralization, privacy, and self-sovereignty. However, this commitment comes with the responsibility to become custodians of our security, to embrace the learning curve, and to navigate the freedoms and duties that define the non-custodial experience. This paradigm encapsulates the spirit of the cryptocurrency movement, offering a pathway to a future where financial autonomy and privacy are paramount.

⬡ Investment Options

Embarking on the cryptocurrency investment journey can lead you to a realm of opportunities, where the allure of digital assets calls for both the seasoned and the novice. This venture into the digital currency landscape can be navigated through direct and indirect pathways, each offering a unique perspective and engagement level with the burgeoning asset class.

Direct Investment

The essence of direct investment lies in the hands-on acquisition and management of cryptocurrencies. Picture yourself engaging in the quintessential act of buying and holding various digital currencies, a strategy affectionately known within the community as "HODLing" (HOLD – holding on for dear life). This approach is akin to planting seeds in a digital garden, where assets like Bitcoin, Ethereum, or an array of altcoins are nurtured with the hope that they will flourish over time.

For the thrill-seekers and market mavens, trading cryptocurrencies presents an electrifying arena. Armed with market knowledge and an appetite for risk, traders navigate the ebbs and flows of digital asset prices, aiming to capitalize on short-term movements. Whether it is the rapid-fire exchanges of day trading or the strategic maneuvers of swing trading, the market's volatility offers fertile ground for potential gains.

Venturing further into the frontier, initial coin offerings (ICOs) and token sales emerge as gateways to early-stage investment opportunities. Here, investors have the chance to back projects at their inception, acquiring tokens before they hit the broader market. While the allure of high returns is tempting, it is paired with the stark reality that not all projects reach their promised potential, weaving a tapestry of risk and reward.

Beyond mere acquisition, the digital domain offers innovative earning mechanisms through staking and yield farming. These methods invite participants to lock up their tokens, contributing to network liquidity or security, and in return, harvest additional tokens as rewards. It's a dynamic way to engage with the DeFi ecosystem, marrying investment with active participation.

Indirect Investment

For those looking to tread lightly or diversify their exposure, indirect investment channels serve as bridges to the digital asset world. Cryptocurrency funds stand out as conduits, allowing investors to tap into the digital asset market without the intricacies of direct management. Whether through index funds mirroring the performance of a crypto ensemble or actively managed portfolios, these funds present a curated path to digital asset investment.

The blockchain and crypto-related stock market offer another layer of engagement. By investing in companies tethered to blockchain technology or those with significant crypto holdings, investors gain a stake in the sector's growth without direct cryptocurrency ownership. It's a strategy that marries the traditional stock market's familiarity with the innovative zest of the crypto and blockchain arena.

Exchange-Traded Funds (ETFs) and crypto trusts introduce further dimensions of indirect investment, offering shares that reflect the value of underlying digital assets. These instruments provide a blend of traditional market accessibility with cryptocurrency exposure, encapsulating the digital assets' essence within more familiar investment vehicles.

Lastly, the broader blockchain technology investment spectrum opens. Beyond the currencies themselves lies the foundational tech—blockchain—that powers these digital assets. Investing in this technology, whether through startups pioneering innovative solutions or established firms integrating blockchain into their operations, offers a visionary angle on the crypto phenomenon.

Alternative Investment

When exploring alternative onramps for dipping your toes into the cryptocurrency waters, PayPal and Cash App stand out, each with its unique set of features tailored to different user needs. PayPal makes it easy for those new to the crypto scene, allowing the purchase, sale, and holding of four major players: Bitcoin, Ethereum, Litecoin, and Bitcoin Cash, all within the safety of its ecosystem. However, it's worth noting that PayPal keeps things in-house, meaning you won't be moving your crypto assets to external wallets or making payments with them outside its platform. Security is top-notch, with two-factor authentication and encryption at the helm, though keep an eye on varying transaction fees based on market activity.

On the flip side, Cash App broadens the horizon with a wider selection of cryptocurrencies, including the likes of Dogecoin, and steps up with the ability to transfer cryptocurrencies to other users or even pay at certain merchants, offering a bit more freedom for those looking to use crypto more actively. While Cash App also prioritizes security, some users voice concerns over its robustness compared to PayPal. The fee structure here is a bit more straightforward, charging a flat 2% on transactions.

Choosing between PayPal and Cash App might boil down to your crypto engagement level. PayPal is a solid choice for those sticking to basic transactions within a secure, contained environment. In contrast, Cash App caters to users seeking more flexibility in their crypto dealings, despite slightly higher fees and discussions around security. Remember, the crypto market is known for its volatility, so arm yourself with thorough research and a clear understanding of the risks before making any investment. This overview isn't financial advice but rather a guide to help you navigate your options between PayPal and Cash App's cryptocurrency features.

As you chart your course through the cryptocurrency investment landscape, whether directly hands-on or through indirect channels, the journey is punctuated with considerations of risk, research, and strategic planning. The volatile nature of digital assets, paired with their innovative potential, crafts a narrative of opportunity tempered with caution. As the crypto and blockchain narrative unfolds, the pathways to participation are as diverse as the investors who walk them, each finding their rhythm in the digital finance dance.

⬡ Building on a Solid Foundation

As we close this chapter on the foundational aspects of cryptocurrencies and blockchain technology, it's clear the journey doesn't end here. The landscape of digital currencies and blockchain is vast and continually evolving, presenting endless opportunities for further exploration and growth. Here's how one might consider advancing their journey into this innovative realm:

After laying down a solid foundation, the next steps involve diving deeper into the practical, educational, and communal facets of the blockchain world. Begin by engaging in actual crypto transactions or trading on various platforms to gain firsthand experience. Explore the decentralized finance (DeFi) ecosystem and experiment with decentralized applications (DApps) to understand their functionalities and potential.

For those with a technical inclination, learning to program in blockchain-specific languages such as Solidity opens up the intricate world of smart contracts and DApp development. Contributing to or initiating blockchain projects can not only bolster your understanding but also connect you with the industry's cutting edge.

Immersing yourself in blockchain and cryptocurrency communities, including leveraging the rich resources available through Grow My Bag, offers a unique pathway to deepening your knowledge and expanding your network within the industry. Engaging with Grow My Bag's social community allows you to connect with like-minded individuals and professionals, fostering valuable discussions and insights. Their comprehensive suite of articles and courses provides a structured approach to learning, from basic concepts to advanced strategies in blockchain and cryptocurrency. Additionally, Grow My Bag's knowledgebase serves as a critical tool for staying updated on the latest trends, research, and developments in this rapidly evolving domain. This blend of community engagement and continuous education is essential for anyone looking to remain informed and relevant in the fast-paced world of digital currencies and blockchain technology.

Delving into the regulatory, ethical, and financial strategies surrounding blockchain and cryptocurrencies will equip you with a well-rounded perspective necessary for responsible participation and investment in the space. Expanding your view to understand the global adoption and regulation landscape of blockchain technology can unveil insights into future trends and opportunities.

Integrating these next steps into your blockchain journey not only enriches your understanding but also prepares you for active and informed participation in the cryptocurrency ecosystem. Whether your interest lies in technological innovation, investment, or contributing to the blockchain community, these steps pave the way for a deeper engagement and potential opportunities in the evolving world of digital currencies and blockchain technology.

This progression from foundational knowledge to deeper involvement and specialization in the blockchain space underscores a journey of continuous learning and exploration. As you navigate through these next steps, remember that the blockchain realm is one of constant change and innovation, offering endless possibilities for those willing to delve deeper and contribute to its growth.

⬡ Acronym Quick Reference

2FA–Two-Factor Authentication
A security process in which a user provides two different authentication factors to verify their identity. This can include something the user knows (e.g., a password), something the user has (e.g., a smartphone), or something the user is (e.g., a fingerprint).

AI–Artifical Intelligence
AI is essentially intelligence displayed by machines, enabling them to learn, reason, and solve problems like humans.

AML–Anti-money Laundering
Anti-money laundering (AML) refers to a set of laws, regulations, and procedures that are designed to prevent, detect, and report money laundering activities. Money laundering is the process of disguising the proceeds of illegal activities as legitimate funds, and AML measures are intended to disrupt this process and prevent the illicit use of financial systems.

AR–Augmented Reality
Augmented reality (AR) is a technology that superimposes computer-generated graphics, sounds, or other digital information onto the real world in real-time. AR can be experienced through various devices, such as smartphones, tablets, or specialized glasses, and is often used in gaming, entertainment, education, and other applications.

CEX–Centralized Exchange
A centralized exchange (CEX) is a digital asset exchange that is operated and controlled by a single entity or organization. CEXs typically offer a range of services, including trading, deposit and withdrawal of digital assets, and sometimes custody of assets on behalf of users. In contrast to decentralized exchanges (DEXs), which are operated and governed by a distributed network of nodes or participants, CEXs are typically more centralized and may be subject to greater regulatory oversight and security risks.

dApps–Decentralized Applications

Decentralized applications are applications that run on a decentralized network, such as the Bitcoin blockchain. Bitcoin DApps use smart contracts to automate processes and enforce rules and are designed to be trustless and transparent. Examples of Bitcoin DApps include exchanges, prediction markets, and games.

DeFi–Decentralized Finance

DeFi, or decentralized finance, refers to financial services and products that are built on decentralized technologies, such as blockchain, and operate without the need for a central authority. DeFi includes a wide range of financial services, such as lending, borrowing, trading, and payment processing.

DEX–Decentralized Exchange

A cryptocurrency exchange that operates in a decentralized manner, meaning it does not rely on a central authority to facilitate trades. Instead, trades are facilitated directly between users using smart contracts. DEXs offer greater security and privacy compared to centralized exchanges but may have lower liquidity and slower trade speeds.

DPINs–Decentralized Physical Infrastructure Networks

Decentralized Physical Infrastructure Networks (DPINs) refer to systems where the control and operation of critical infrastructure—such as energy grids, water systems, telecommunications, and transportation networks—are not centralized under a single entity or authority. Instead, they are distributed across multiple nodes, which could be individuals, communities, or small organizations that collectively manage and operate the infrastructure.

ETH–Ether

This is the native cryptocurrency of the Ethereum blockchain. It is used to pay for transaction fees on the network and can also be used as a form of digital payment.

HODL–Hold On for Dear Life
A slang term in the cryptocurrency community that means to hold onto a cryptocurrency rather than sell it. The term originated from a typo in a forum post in which the user meant to type hold but instead wrote HODL.

IoT–Internet of Things
The Internet of Things (IoT) refers to the interconnected network of physical objects (e.g., devices, vehicles, buildings) that are embedded with sensors, software, and network connectivity, enabling them to collect and exchange data.

KYC–Know Your Customer
A process in which a business or organization verifies the identity of its clients and assesses their potential risks for money laundering or financing terrorism. In the context of cryptocurrency, KYC processes are often used by exchanges to ensure compliance with anti-money laundering regulations.

MACD–Moving Average Convergence Divergence
A technical analysis indicator that measures the difference between two moving averages and is used to identify trend changes and generate buy and sell signals.

MR–Mixed Reality
Mixed reality blends the physical world you see around you with computer-generated elements. It's like having a transparent computer screen where virtual objects appear to coexist and interact with real-world objects. Unlike virtual reality (VR) which completely immerses you in a simulated environment, MR allows you to see and interact with both the real and virtual worlds simultaneously.

NFT–Non-fungible Token
A Non-fungible Token (NFT) can be thought of as a unique digital certificate of ownership for a digital or physical asset.

PoH–Proof-of-History (PoH)
A technique for securely recording the existence and order of events in a distributed system. PoH can be used to establish a verifiable record of events without requiring a central authority or trusted third party.

PoS–Proof-of-Stake (PoS)
A consensus mechanism in which the validator of the next block is chosen based on their stake (how many coins they hold) in the blockchain. In PoS, the probability of a validator being chosen to create a block is proportional to their stake in the blockchain.

RSI–Relative Strength Index (RSI)
A technical indicator that measures the strength of a security's price action by comparing the magnitude of recent gains to recent losses.

SSI–Self-Sovereign Identity
SSI hands users the keys to their digital identity, enabling control over personal data and online credentials without relying on central authorities.

SSL–Secure Sockets Layer
Secure Sockets Layer is a cryptographic protocol that ensures secure communication between a web browser and a website. It essentially creates an encrypted tunnel to protect any data exchanged between the two.

USDC–USD Coin
USD Coin is a type of cryptocurrency known as a stablecoin and is pegged to the US dollar. To maintain this stability, USDC is backed by reserves of real US dollars or equivalent assets held by regulated financial institutions.

USDT–USDT or Tether
USDT or Tether, is a type of cryptocurrency known as a stablecoin. It is algorithmically pegged to the US dollar.

VR–Virual Reality

Virtual reality (VR) is a technology that creates an immersive and interactive experience that simulates a user's physical presence in a computer-generated world.

XRP–XRP

XRP is a cryptocurrency used on the XRP Ledger, a blockchain network designed for fast and cheap international payments. Think of it like a digital bridge currency that helps move money between countries quickly and with lower fees.

⬡ About the Author

Eddie Johnson's entrepreneurial journey began in elementary school with the launch of an errand business, showcasing his innate ability to recognize and seize opportunities. As the visionary founder of Rebel Visions Corporation for more than two decades, Eddie has delivered expert consulting services to numerous Fortune 500 companies. Seeking to broaden his firm's impact, he initiated a digital marketing division, Rebel Reach, which quickly set itself apart by weaving Web3 and AI technologies into the ecommerce and content development realms.

Eddie's drive for innovation continued to flourish. Having advised clients on the benefits of podcasting, he took his own advice and started "Eddie Jay on Crypto." This podcast aimed not only to share his investment journey but also to instill his work ethic and innovative spirit in his children in a engaging manner. This personal endeavor soon transformed into "Grow My Bag™," a platform that broadens the dialogue to encompass a wide array of investment and business insights for an expanding audience.

"Grow My Bag™" has emerged as a vibrant social media ecosystem, captivating audiences with diverse content across social site, notably the Grow My Bag social media platform. Eddie's commitment and adaptability have not only positioned him as a thought leader but also inspired many to request his expertise in educational classes. Meeting this demand, Eddie has crafted class content, leading to the creation of this book.

Eddie's transition from a youthful entrepreneur to a distinguished figure in the digital and management consulting fields exemplifies his remarkable business insight and dedication to knowledge sharing. In this book, Eddie extends an invitation to readers to delve into the essentials of cryptocurrency and more, sharing the wisdom of a lifetime marked by innovation and achievement.

⬡ The Metaverse Standards Forum

The Metaverse Standards Forum stands at the forefront of shaping the Metaverse, a burgeoning domain of interconnected virtual experiences. As a Principal Member, Rebel Visions Corporation, steered by Eddie's vision, engages actively in this collaborative effort. The Forum serves as a cooperative arena, uniting standards organizations, industry leaders, and open-source innovators. It aims to synchronize efforts and expedite the establishment of interoperable frameworks within the Metaverse, paving the way for a wave of business opportunities and user-centric experiences.

Acting as a facilitator rather than a standards creator, the Forum provides a neutral ground for consensus-building on technical requirements, ensuring broad adoption and visibility of initiatives. Open to any entity willing to contribute, it offers free membership tiers to encourage diverse participation and a hands-on approach to tackle immediate interoperability challenges. Frequent and ongoing discussions within the Forum highlight a pragmatic and responsive methodology, deeply connected to real-world industry needs.

In this inclusive and action-oriented setting, Rebel Visions Corporation contributes to a collective mission: constructing the Metaverse as an accessible, efficient, and comprehensive digital environment. By aligning with the Forum's goals, the company not only stays abreast of emerging Metaverse dynamics but also positions itself as an integral player in realizing a coherent vision for this revolutionary digital frontier.

⬡ Notes

⬡ Notes

⬡ **Notes**